Everything You to Know to Structure Your Business

Troy Anders

Published by
Anders Publishing
4830 Wilson Road Suite 156
Humble, TX 77396

•

•

ISBN 9781648586606

Everything You Need to Know to Structure Your Business was composed to assist individuals with the necessary steps to build a solid business foundation that could last for decades. Starting a business is an exciting time in one's life. Often times, businesses are started to make a quick dollar, while others are started to begin generational wealth. Whichever reason it is you are starting your business; we wish you the best.

We want you to know that hard work and dedication are a major part of the success of your business. Distinctive characteristics make an effective business owner and entrepreneur. While a successful business is determined by many measures, it starts with a solid foundation. The information provided in ***Everything You Need to Know to Structure Your Business*** will make it easy for you to understand the process of structuring a business and always keeps you in charge of your business. Follow the steps below and watch your business grow!

So, you have decided to start a business. This is GREAT! The next question is, what kind of business? It is always wise to start a business in which you have the experience, expertise, and or resources. Not having a clear image of your business will have you trapped in the world of possibilities and finished before you start. Choosing the type of business, you want is the most important part of starting a business. Starting a business, you have a passion for is always a plus. It is said, "If you love what you do, you'll never work a day in your life." I like to say to Package Your Passion and Profit!

You will have to know if your business is Non-Profit or For-Profit. You will also have to determine if your business is an online business (virtual store, information source, etc.), retail storefront, personal service provider, etc.

A few questions to ask yourself to determine which type of business you will start are as follows:

What is the purpose of my business?
How will I fund this venture?
How will I generate revenue?
Will I need employees?

Once you have answered those questions, it is time to determine how to effectively structure your business. There are several ways to structure your business and it is my pleasure to layout each of them while explaining the advantages and disadvantages.

Each state has different forms and fees while others are standard across the US. If you are need of further information as well as assistance in structuring your business, you can send all your business concerns and needs to info@andersconsultinggroup.com

Sole Proprietorship

Sole Proprietorship Advantages

Sole Proprietorship Disadvantages

Partnerships

Types of Partnerships

Forming a Partnership

Filing information for Partnerships

Partnership Advantages

Partnership Disadvantages

Corporations

Corporation Advantages

Corporation Disadvantages

S Corporation

S Corporation Advantages

S Corporation Disadvantages

C Corporation

C Corporation Advantages

C Corporation Disadvantages

Limited Liability Company

Limited Liability Company Advantages

Limited Liability Company Disadvantages

Non-Profit Organization

Types of Non-profit Organizations

Non-Profit 501(c)(1)

Non-Profit 501(c)(2)

Non-Profit 501(c)(2)

Non-Profit 501(c)(3)

The types of 501(c)(3) organizations:

Non-Profit 501(c)(5)

501(c)(8) - Fraternal Societies

501(c)(9) - Employee Beneficiary Association

501(c)(11) - Teacher's Retirement Fund Associations

501(c)(13) - Cemetery Companies

501(c)(14) - State Chartered Credit Union and Mutual Reserve Fund

501(c)(15) - Mutual Insurance Companies of Association

____

____

____

____

____

____

____

501(c)(17) - Supplemental Unemployment Benefits Trust

____

____

____

____

____

____

501(c)(18) - Employee Funded Pension Trust

501(c)(19) - Veterans Organizations

Non-Profit 501(c)(20)

501(c)(22) - Withdrawal Liability Payment Fund

501(c)(23) - Veterans Organization

501(c)(26) - State-Sponsored Organizations Providing Coverage for High-Risk Individuals

501(c)(27) - State-Sponsored Workers' Compensation Reinsurance Organizations

501(d) - Religious and Apostolic Associations

501(e) - Cooperative Hospital Service Organizations

Non-profit Organization Advantages

Non-Profit Organization Disadvantages

Naming Your Business

Search the Availability of Your Business Name

Register Your Business Name with State

Register Your Assumed Name with The Secretary of State

When Do You Need a "DBA"?
(Doing Business As)

How to Register Your "DBA" Name

Difference Between Assumed Name and DBA

Register for Your EIN or Federal Tax ID with the IRS

How to Apply for an EIN?

Register Your Business with Dunn and Bradstreet

Business Certifications

Register Your Business with the 8(a) Business Development Program

Benefits of the 8(a) Business Development Program

8(a) Business Development Program Requirements

Trademark Your Business Name and Logo

Registering Your Business Name as a Trademark

Trademark Disadvantages

Registering Your Logo as a Trademark

Types of Business Taxes

Income Tax:

Direct Costs:

Indirect Costs:

Service Costs:

Capital Expenses

Personal versus Business Expenses:

Using Your Home for Business:

Using Your Car for Business

Other Business Expenses

Payroll

Retirement Plans:

Rent Expense:

Interest Expense:

Taxes:

____

____

____

____

____

____

____

____

Insurance:

____

____

____

____

____

Business Plan

What Makes a Strong Business Plan?

Executive Summary

Mission Statement:

____

____

____

____

____

Company Information:

____

____

____

____

Growth Highlights:

____

____

____

____

Products/Services:

____

____

____

____

Financial Information:

____

____

____

____

Summarize the future:

What if You Are a Start-up or New Business:

Company Description

Company Description should include:

Market Analysis

Market Analysis should include:

Industry:

____

____

____

____

Know Your Target Market:

____

____

____

____

____

____

____

____

____

____

____

____

____

____

____

____

____

____

____

____

Market share:

Regulatory Provisions:

Organization & Management

Board of Directors':

Service or Product Line

Service or Product Line

Description of Your Product / Service

Intellectual Property:

Marketing Strategy

Funding Request

Financial Projections:

Appendix

The Appendix should include:

Printed in the USA
CPSIA information can be obtained
at www.ICGtesting.com
CBHW081555011124
16777CB00009B/835